C000217536

RUNNING OUT OF STEAM

A few reminders of some of the stations that have played second home to me over these last few years.

RUNNING OUT OF STEAM

The photographic diary
of a teenage railway enthusiast,
1966-68

David Mather

Foreword by Ian Allan OBE

Silver Link Publishing Ltd

For Mair, for her help, encouragement and patience

© David Mather 2010

All rights reserved. No part of this publication may be reproduced, stored in a retrieval system or transmitted, in any form or by any means, electronic, mechanical, photocopying, recording or otherwise, without prior permission in writing from Silver Link Publishing Ltd.

First published in 2010

British Library Cataloguing in Publication Data

A catalogue record for this book is available from the British Library.

ISBN 978 1 85794 326 9

Silver Link Publishing Ltd
The Trundle
Ringstead Road
Great Addington
Kettering
Northants NN14 4BW

Tel/Fax: 01536 330588
email: sales@nostalgiacollection.com
Website: www.nostalgiacollection.com

Printed and bound in the Czech Republic

CONTENTS

PREFACE

This is my photographic recollection of some of my experiences at the trackside during the final years of steam haulage on Britain's railways, which, luckily for me, centred on the Manchester/Bolton area and the nearby West Coast Main Line.

All photographs were taken by me unless otherwise stated. All information is correct and as accurate as my notes and memory allow.

David Mather, Bolton, August 1968

The view I came to know and love: the so-called 'Orlando Bridge' was next to Bolton East signal box, here looking towards Trinity Street station, with the imposing structure of the London Midland & Scottish goods warehouse to the right of the station. From an early age my long-suffering mother would bring me here to watch the expresses and the constant shunting of the saddle tanks in the sidings that overlooked the home of Bolton Wanderers, Burnden Park.

FOREWORD

by Ian Allan OBE

A lot of water has flowed under a lot of bridges since that fateful November 1942 when the *ABC of Southern Locomotives* was launched on an unsuspecting public, and an excited Ian Allan laid wait for Corquodales (the Southern Railway's printer), who made a daily visit to the Southern's public relations department. The wrong chap arrived and what followed was part of a general serendipity and led me on to a love of railways and becoming a publisher by accident.

Prior to 1942 the railway enthusiast had no real way of finding out the details of the locomotives he saw, and it must have been something of a pleasant shock when he found himself able to find the minutest detail of names and numbers and the principal dimensions of every engine in the fleet – and for only 2 shillings a throw.

The *ABC of Southern Locomotives* was the first in a series that ran to millions of copies during the heyday of railway enthusiasm. It was virtually inevitable that the other big three railway companies would be covered similarly to the Southern, and out came not only more detailed railway books, but 'spotting' books for buses, aircraft, trams – in fact, any form of moving transport.

It was not beer and skittles all the way. Mr Bulleid, the Southern's CME, got pretty hot under the collar when a book about *his* locomotives was published without his knowledge. The *ABC of LMS Locomotives* appeared in court for the prosecution of boys who, bored at seeing the same locomotives in the Birmingham area, took themselves to a convenient spot in Tamworth where they placed pennies on the line to see which locomotives would squash them best.

In the course of more than 60 years in publishing many opportunities were taken, some with disastrous results, but that's publishing – there is nothing less valuable than a clean sheet of paper once something has been printed on it!

Getting into print is not as easy as it looks, but it is good that Mr Mather has recalled so graphically and nostalgically the trains of yesteryear we loved so much, but alas no one can stop the advance of technology that makes trains go not at 60mph but up to 200mph. The trouble is, they go so fast that you can't read the station signs, and the locomotives are so standard that one tends to dismiss them all as being the same.

But there is hope yet as whistles blow and engines puff. On the successors to the big railways – the heritage railways of Britain – steam still abounds, services are being increased and great enthusiasm is raised among the younger generation who never saw the real thing but now have a jolly good substitute, with 100 or more systems operating in almost every county in the kingdom.

Running Out Of Steam is sad, but surely interest will grow as new trains, new stations, new rails and new signalling systems are introduced to herald the beginnings of a super railway in the years ahead.

INTRODUCTION

The beginning of the end

The late 1950s saw the introduction of main-line diesels on a large scale – English Electric Type 4s, British Railways 'Peaks', and the diesel-hydraulic 'Warships'. In addition, a multitude of multiple units were soon replacing the branch-line steam classes that had served so well for so long. Later, there followed the more powerful 'Western' Class and the mighty 'Deltics', together with a host of 'Brush' and 'Metro-Vick' engines, which are still being built to this day. Although welcomed at first, the novelty of the diesels was soon to wear off, and enthusiasts began to mourn the loss of their steam engines.

As the number of E-E Type 4 and, later, Brush diesels increased, and these began taking charge of the crack expresses, the larger 'Pacifics' – the 'Duchesses' and the 'Princess Royals' – were of course made redundant. But although this marked the end of the line for the 'Princess Royals', it was not quite so for their rather younger cousins. The 'Princess Royal' Class locos, introduced in 1933 and 1935, were lighter and smaller engines than the 'Coronation' Class, or 'Duchesses', even though they could develop a slightly greater tractive effort. But the latter, introduced mainly in 1937, had the important advantage of more modern thinking, which resulted in the development of new techniques of boiler and cylinder internal streamlining, to allow the greatest possible amounts of steam to be utilised more speedily and more efficiently than on earlier 'Pacifics' of Stanier design.

Therefore the 'Duchesses' were still an economic proposition, though no longer needed in charge of major long-haul expresses such as the 'Royal Scot', as in the past,

9

A Class 47 diesel takes its train away from Bolton towards Preston, along the Deane Clough route.

The impressive semaphores guarding Burnden Junction allow a DMU from Manchester Victoria to approach Bolton Trinity Street station.

except in an emergency. More usually, the last days of these mighty engines were spent hauling express freights, such as perishable foods like freshly caught fish from the great ports to the markets, especially to London, in the shortest possible time. Thus the conveyance of perishable freight, at speeds often greater than the express passenger trains, became the final task of the mighty 'Duchess' 'Pacifics', but it was plain to all that their days were strictly numbered.

Within two years it had become obvious what was happening. Few minded the quite painless removal of a few dirty old tank engines, and even the 'Compounds' and curious 'Crabs' were seemingly not missed, but by 1962 the matter had become much more serious. The winter 1962/63 edition of Ian Allan's *abc British Railways Locomotives* 'Combined Volume' (now incidentally increased in price from 10s 6d to 11s 6d) carried within its pages a sad sight for railway enthusiasts. About half of the 'Patriot' Class had been withdrawn, including class leader No 45500 *Patriot*, together with six of the twelve 'Princess Royals'. A shock indeed, but worse was to come. Within five short years, steam haulage on British Railways was to be reduced to nil.

I take up the story now in 1966, after an absence of nearly five years from the trackside. My interest in steam engines was reborn in June 1966, while on holiday at Butlins Holiday Camp, Pwllheli, North Wales, for here Mr (later Sir) Billy Butlin had preserved two steam locomotives that had been doomed by British Railways shortly before. These two engines were 'Princess' Class No 46203 *Princess Margaret Rose* and Southern Region 'A1X' 0-6-0 tank No 32640, which had been withdrawn from service with the closure of the Havant to Hayling Island line. The majesty of the steam engine served to fan the flame that had lain dormant.

Thus it was that during the winter of 1966-67 I made my first journey for five years to watch trains.

'Princess' 'Pacific' No 46203 *Princess Margaret Rose* and ex-LB&SCR 'A1X' 0-6-0T No 32640 at Butlins, Pwllheli.

An idea of the size of the 'Pacific' can be clearly appreciated, as the driving wheels stand 6ft 6in high, and the engine's weight is 104.5 tons.

1967

SPRING

Back on track again

A friend and I travel up to Preston from Bolton by road, then continue from Preston to Lancaster by rail. It is a terrible day, cold and wet, the light gloomy and the atmosphere heavy.

Nevertheless, this train journey is my first for so long that, in spite of speed restrictions necessitated by newly laid track, the feeling is one that brings back many happy memories. Fellow passengers are left in a state of amazement by my attempts to photograph a 'Britannia' as she passes at speed, pushing through the driving rain. The atmosphere at Lancaster station is wet and dismal, and few steam trains come through. We wait all afternoon. At last signals are raised for what turns out to be the only steam-hauled train to reward our patience. Through the poor light and constant drizzle emerges one of the remaining 8F 2-8-0s hauling its heavy freight southbound.

Spring at last

The advent of spring 1967, and better conditions for photographing trains, finds me on a trip to Poole in Dorset, as part of a geography field week from school. That Easter saw the last of the 'Battle of Britain' and 'West Country' Class engines still operating in the area, though living on borrowed time.

Above: Waiting for steam trains: Lancaster Castle station.

Below: A snatched shot of one of the surviving 'Pacifics' approaching Poole on 20 March 1967.

Above: In the border country; while on Shap station I am lucky enough to be rewarded by the passing of a southbound fitted freight hauled by one of the surviving class 9F 2-10-0 locomotives, No 92106.

Below: 9F No 92009 heads north through Penrith.

Meanwhile, on the London Midland Region steam can now only be found working between Crewe and Carlisle, so I am fortunate to live between these two railway centres, and not too far from the West Coast Main Line. Of the two great summits that the crack expresses of the West Coast Main Line have to climb, Shap and Beattock, only on Shap can steam still be seen and, while travelling up to Scotland on holiday in June of this year, I could not resist stopping off for a look. The old station, which has seen the 'Royal Scot' thunder past hauled by a shining red or green 'Coronation' Class engine, with as many as 18 coaches behind (and often reaching the summit unaided) still stands to witness the last steam-hauled trains – still rarely aided by banker engines.

From Shap I travel on northwards to Penrith, where, after a wait of over an hour, I photograph 9F No 92209 with a fitted goods train travelling towards Carlisle after successfully bringing its heavy load over Shap Summit. This engine, like so many others left in service, has been relieved of its smokebox number plate and shed plate, but has at least been provided with a piece of black-painted wood bearing its number

Beyond Carlisle

By the time we reach Carlisle it is too dark to take photographs, though many subjects are worthy of recording in the evening lights of Citadel station, including 'Britannia' Class No 70011 *Hotspur*, one of several of her class shedded here.

The following morning sees us travelling northwards once more, so no more steam engines for the time being. However, a visit to Beattock station cannot be resisted and, although trains of any description are few and far between, we smile wryly at the 'progress' that has taken place since the end of steam haulage over the summit.

By 30 June 1967 English Electric Type 1s have taken over banking duties in the area and are used to haul lighter goods trains, although on this occasion the subject fails to reach the summit and has to wait for a sister engine to give her a shove up to the top!

An uncomfortable and largely sleepless night in Beattock station waiting room is to follow, with only the passing E-E Type 4s and 'Peaks' providing interest. However, the scene is now set, and through the summer and autumn of 1967 the West Coast Main Line is to become a second home.

MAY

The weekends are spoken for. The West Coast Main Line is the place to be for as long as steam can hold out. Wigan North Western, Preston and Lancaster Castle stations are set to become as familiar to me as the lines in and out of Bolton Trinity Street were years ago. Then it was my mum who kept a watchful eye over my early trainspotting Saturday afternoons. Now, in my late teens, my friend and I travel almost weekly to see the dwindling stock of survivors.

Weekends can't come along fast enough now, as the weather warms and days on cold, wet railway stations become expeditions into the comfortable glow of summer afternoons.

'Britannia' Class No 70045 *Lord Rowallan* heads north through Lancaster Castle station with a fitted freight train, before these last few were returned to passenger duties for the summer holiday 'specials'.

Above: A Stanier Class 5 waits at the signals at Lancaster with a northbound parcels train, while a 'Brush' diesel hurries south with an express passenger service.

Right: 'Britannia' Class No 70010 *Owen Glendower* defeats my camera as it races southbound through Wigan North Western station.

Right: Class 9F No 92010 passes through Wigan with a southbound freight.

Above: Class 8F No 48371 passes through Lancaster Castle station in May 1967 with a northbound freight, while waiting in the background is a DMU for Bare Lane and Morecambe Promenade.

Below: Steam at Wigan North Western in May 1967: two 'Black Fives' wait to enter the main line with northbound freight trains. Careful positioning allows the drivers to chat before one of them moves on.

Class 9F No 92128 passes Lancaster station with a southbound train of Shell-BP petroleum wagons in May 1967.

JUNE

Pause for thought

On a subsequent visit to Preston station, I have the opportunity to look at a recent edition of Ian Allan's 'Combined Volume', now sold at the outrageous price of 12s 6d! To my surprise and horror, I find that there are practically no steam locomotives operating outside the London Midland Region. Even on the LMR, the only named engines still in service are the remaining 'Britannias', and even these have had all their identification plates (number, name and shed) removed, ostensibly to foil collectors with spanners. Some of the class have had their names and numbers painted on again at Carlisle shed, and a welcome sight this is too.

Other steam locos still operating include 'Black Fives', 8Fs, some BR Standard 2MT 2-6-0s and some BR Standard 4MT and 5MT 4-6-0s, together with quite a few 9Fs. Very little else!

In recent weeks I have been privileged to travel behind several of the remaining 'Britannia' Class locos, including Nos 70010 *Owen Glendower*, 70012 *John of Gaunt*, 70023 *Venus*, 70038 *Robin Hood* and 70045 *Lord Rowallan*. In addition, several of my journeys have been hauled by the once ubiquitous 'Black Fives', still performing well after all these years.

At the present time, the summer holiday traffic is in operation, and as a result several 'Britannia' Class engines have been given a final clean-up and returned to passenger service to haul holiday specials between Crewe and Carlisle, most frequently on Barrow trains.

Steam-hauled expresses are very rare today, and can only be found on this section of the LMR, and even here only on summer Saturdays. One notable exception is the daily steam-hauled service that pauses at Bolton shortly after 9 o'clock every evening. It is the 'Belfast Boat Express' for Heysham Harbour. This is usually pulled by a 'Black Five' engine, invariably in excellent mechanical condition and with an enthusiastic crew on board! Acceleration and braking are breathtaking, as the driver and fireman race for the coast. Occasionally this service has been entrusted to 'Britannia' No 70023 *Venus*, but with disappointing results in terms of clocked times, arriving at Heysham several minutes late. Plans are afoot to ride this express on a regular basis in the near future, boarding at Bolton and staying on to Preston or Lancaster, perhaps remaining there overnight, then returning with it the following afternoon en route to Manchester.

Briefly leaving steam

Recent visits outside the region have had mixed results. A trip to the East Coast Main Line proved somewhat better than I had anticipated, especially the splendour of York, in spite of the now total absence of steam traction, but a visit to Crewe was singularly unrewarding. Grantham was worth the long drive, though. Here the powerful 'Deltics' shake the station in much the same way that the 'A4s' and their cousins must have done not so long ago. The sheer power of the 'Deltics' travelling at speed makes them an exciting spectacle, almost, but not quite, in the same league as steam power!

Also in June 1967 I travel to Scotland, and take the opportunity to spend a while on Edinburgh station. Here the 'Deltics' take on a much more subdued appearance, yet the roar of their engines as they move off must surely be one of the most distinctive sounds on the railways.

Above: Some years after my first encounter with 'Deltics', No 55010 *The Kings Own Scottish Borderer* (No D9010 in 1967) threads through York station with the 10.00am Kings Cross to Edinburgh non-stop service – the 'Flying Scotsman' – and bang on time!

Below: Also at York, No 55020 *Nimbus* (the former D9020) departs with the northbound *Aberdonian*.

JULY

Back on the WCML

On Saturday 29 July we spend much of the day travelling the West Coast Main Line between Preston and Lancaster, making three return trips. Of these six journeys, three are steam-hauled, two are hauled by 'Brush 4' diesels and one, unfortunately, by diesel multiple unit! Of the three steam-hauled runs we have, the first is with a 'Black Five', which constantly throws out clouds of black smoke containing unusually large lumps of very hot coal. One lump strikes the window where I am standing. It leaves an impression in the frame that makes me glad I had temporarily withdrawn from my customary 'head out of the window' position. The other two steam runs are provided by 'Britannias' with their expert crews. Driver and fireman must work as one to coax the best from these grand old ladies, and combine their skills to raise the maximum steam from ageing boilers.

First was No 70038 *Robin Hood*, north from Preston to Lancaster. She still looks good after being cleaned up earlier in the month to take a Stephenson Locomotive Society special from Birmingham, taking over from an electric loco on the leg from Stockport to York. After somewhat limited success photographing *Robin Hood* and sister engine No 70024 *Vulcan* through clouds of steam, it is time to climb aboard and depart for Lancaster.

We have not been at Lancaster very long when we are rewarded with the arrival of another 'Brit', again with a special passenger train.

Left: Wreathed in steam, waiting to depart from Preston for Lancaster, 'Britannia' Class No 70038 *Robin Hood* (*above*) is joined by sister engine No 70024 *Vulcan*.

Below: Venus continues her journey south from Preston. Note that her name plate and shed plate are missing and that a wooden smokebox number plate has been substituted for the original.

Above: Venus waits at the signals at Lancaster Castle station, with one of the summer specials that now feature steam once more.

Below: Seen from the leading coach, with clouds of smoke billowing from her chimney, *Venus* makes a spirited departure towards Preston. Meanwhile, a 'Black Five' takes on water before taking her turn to head southwards with another special passenger train.

Above: En route for Preston: a 'Black Five' light engine waits at the signals as we approach the junction.

Right: Back at Preston station again, 'Britannia' No 70028 *Royal Star* passes through with a southbound fitted freight – one of the few 'Brits' not on passenger services on these summer Saturdays.

No 70045 *Lord Rowallan* comes to a halt at Lancaster with a southbound special.

31

Above: A 2-6-4 tank engine leaves Bolton Trinity Street with a local passenger train, while on the left a 'Black Five' enters the station with a westbound service on the Blackpool line.

Below: A close-up of one of the 2-6-4 tanks, which were so common in an around Bolton in the early 1960s. This is No 42656, and is about to be coupled to a set of carriages that she will take out of the station eastwards, while in the background a sister engine waits at the signals before entering the station.

Reminiscing

Amid the excitement generated by a procession of 'Britannias' it is easy to forget that only a very few years ago the steam scene was very different, and much more varied. Bolton in the early 1960s was almost entirely in the grip of steam traction; only a few diesel multiple units and the occasional Type 4 diesel gave any hint of what was to be in the years to come.

In those days it was difficult to find a place on the footbridge at Trinity Street station, because of the multitudes of trainspotters who congregated there. Most of the local trains to Wigan Wallgate, Manchester, Bury and thereabouts, were pulled by grubby tank engines built in 1935. These engines usually pulled between three and eight coaches and were not generally held in high regard by the assembled spotters.

Though these tanks were the most familiar engines at Bolton, many and varied were the other classes that could also be seen on most days. The oldest of these were 2F 0-6-0 saddle tanks, a design that had originally been introduced in 1877 and rebuilt in 1891. These engines were former Lancashire & Yorkshire Railway stock, and were used regularly on shunting duties in Bolton's goods sidings. Another similar engine type, an example of which was shedded at Bolton in those days, was 0F 0-4-0ST No 51232, which was withdrawn and replaced with a diesel shunter in about 1960. A further ex-L&Y engine also shedded at Bolton was 3F 0-6-0 No 52345, introduced in 1889 and pictured here in a sorry state on shed. Commonly known as 'Coffee Pots' due to their simple design for boiling water and making use of the steam similar to that used in the kitchen implement, these engines were in service until about 1963, when they too were replaced by diesel shunters.

Above: Although the old 'Midland Compounds' had been scrapped some years earlier, Bolton shed still housed its share of 4F 0-6-0s during the early 1960s. These engines were a post-Grouping development of the Midland design and totalled 450 in 1962. They had been introduced in 1924 and were used mainly for local goods services and occasionally on shunting duties in the yards that lay just to the east of the station in Bolton.

Below: One of the post-Grouping developments of the old 'Midland Compounds', introduced in 1924: No 44479 leaves Trinity Street station on the Castle Hill line towards Blackburn in the early 1960s.

Above: 'Crab' 2-6-0 No 42732 takes the through line with an eastbound goods train. In the background a 2-6-4 tank engine awaits her next duty.

Below: Another 'Crab', also on goods, enters the station from the west and passes Bolton West signal box. These engines were in service until about the mid-1960s.

Other engines that could regularly be seen at Bolton and whose days were strictly limited included the 5MT 2-6-0s introduced in 1926 and affectionately referred to as 'Crabs', and the 8F ex-War Department 2-8-0s, known to railwaymen and enthusiasts alike as 'Dub-Dees'.

Bolton shed, 26C

The station and its adjacent bridges were a 'happy hunting ground' for enthusiasts of all ages in those days, but a visit to the engine sheds was always something special. A casual approach was taken by the railwaymen to the interest shown in the locomotives, and rarely was any notice taken of 'trespassers' wandering in and out of the lines of 'Black Fives' and their stablemates.

At the same time as this programme of steam withdrawal is going on in Bolton, much more is happening to main-line steam traffic.

By the time the winter of 1962/63 was upon us, half of the 'Patriot' Class 4-6-0s had been withdrawn, including No 45500 *Patriot* herself. A similar fate had befallen some of the beloved 'Princess' Class 'Pacifics', including Nos 46212 *Duchess of Kent* and 46210 *Lady Patricia*.

'Well,' I thought, 'at least we've still got the "Duchesses",' as we called the 'Coronation' Class 'Pacifics'. But I was soon to learn that even these engines, which many considered the best ever, and which became legends for taking on Shap or Beattock with 18 or more coaches without a 'banker' – even these were not to be spared!

Soon after the extermination of the 'Princess' Class in 1966, a notice appeared in *Modern Railways* that must have saddened the heart of every railway enthusiast or spotter who had ever stood and watched in awe as one of these mighty engines roared by. The notice said simply that

At Bolton sheds, Stanier 8F No 48195 is ready for work, while in the background ex-WD 8F 2-8-0 No 90267 awaits its next duty. These engines were introduced in 1943 and are former War Department stock, purchased by British Railways in 1948. They are mainly used for pulling heavy goods trains and quite a few of them are shedded at Bolton to work the coal trains from the nearby pits. In the background is another of the tank engines once so familiar on both local goods and passenger services at Bolton, No 42530. These engines, too, barely saw the mid-1960s. During the first half of that decade the 'scrap line' at Bolton sheds bore witness to the end of an era – the era of steam-hauled local trains would soon be over.

'Coronation' Class No 46234 *Duchess of Abercorn* had been withdrawn from service. Everyone knew, though few dared say it, that it would not be long before they were all gone, and the ticking over of a diesel engine would be the only sound to break the silence that would hang over their grave.

Another blow soon followed – the news that the 'Royal Scot' Class locos were to be relieved of their nameplates, which were to be fitted to new diesels soon to be built. Had they no shame?

It was becoming increasingly clear that the reign of the 'steam kings' was waning and the diesel pretenders were waiting in the wings. At this stage, many enthusiasts gave up. They could not bear to witness 'their engines', which had so proudly headed the 'Royal Scot', 'Mid-day Scot' or 'Caledonian', being torched to pieces in scrapyards throughout the country, and being usurped by purring, bus-like 'commoners'. For some this was indeed the end of a beautiful friendship; for others it was merely the beginning, but for me it meant one thing. It meant I had better get out and about with my camera, or I would be left with only my memories.

Another ex-WD 8F, No 90339, blows off steam as if trying to persuade BR officials that it can still out-muscle the diesels that are rapidly replacing its kind. But it is all in vain. This engine, together with the rest of its enormous class, were all scrapped in or around 1965, their work being taken over initially by Class 5s, 8Fs and 9Fs.

The race is on

So get out and about is what I do, at every opportunity. The first priority is my home ground, Trinity Street station and the nearby engine sheds, to pay homage to the last moments of steam in Bolton, while on the West Coast Main Line, at least until the end of the summer holiday season, steam-hauled passenger services can still be seen regularly and in considerable numbers. And they are seen by a great many 'regulars': men and boys capture treasured images on cine film, tape recorders and still film, images that in future steamless years will rekindle happy memories.

Class 5 No 45304 coasts into Bolton Trinity Street station with an eastbound passenger train, in the days when diesels were the exception rather than the rule. But this engine and many others appeared on what became known as the 'scrap line' at Bolton shed during the summer of 1967.

Above: One of the almost 850 original 'Black Fives', now reduced by about one-third, No 45119 enters Bolton sheds after completing her schedule for the day.

Below: 'Black Five' No 45436 pauses at Bolton Trinity Street with an eastbound passenger train. These engines are becoming a rarity on passenger services now, except on a limited length of the West Coast Main Line.

Sister engine No 44781 has collected coaches from the sidings to the east of the station and has taken them forward for the next train. She is shedded at Bolton and consequently bears the 26C shed code on her smokebox door.

Above: An all-steam scene at Trinity Street: in the foreground is Class 5 No 45436, beyond which is 5MT 'Crab' No 42732 and another Class 5, queuing patiently at the signals.

Below: At the sheds, resplendent Class 8F 2-8-0 No 48195 eagerly awaits her next turn. Originally numbering 665 locos, sadly a much reduced total survives in 1967.

Class 5 No 45206, running light engine, hurries into Trinity Street, while behind tank No 42537 on a local passenger service is held at a signal obscured by the smoke.

Class 5 No 44939 storms out of Trinity Street with a passenger train for Blackpool. Local steam-hauled services of this kind have now all but vanished, being replaced by diesel multiple units. Shortly after this shot was taken, even this line out of the station was pulled up!

AUGUST

On the main line again

It's Saturday 19 August 1967, and we're off up the WCML again. The trip to Preston is by DMU, which, judging by the rattling noises coming from windows and seats, seems about to fall apart before ever delivering us there. There is very little steam on the way up, but 'Britannia' Class No 70024 *Vulcan* brightens the otherwise forgettable trip as she races south with a passenger special.

From Preston we travel on to Lancaster aboard a Manchester-Barrow train hauled energetically by Class 5 No 44709. A Horwich-built 'Black Five' now stabled at Carnforth (10A), she is still giving full value!

From Lancaster it is back south again to Preston, diesel-hauled this time, with a Glasgow-Manchester express. This brings back fond memories of junior school days about eight years ago, when the 'Glazzie' was hauled by a 'Clan', 'Scot' or 'Brit'. Racing out of school at 4 o'clock, friends and I had just about enough time to run down the road and across a park to a spot about 100 yards from the line into Bolton, before the sound of No 72004 *Clan MacDonald*, racing over the distant water troughs, would be ringing in our ears. The signals would be up. We would be sweating and out of breath, but the 'Glazzie' was always worth it. Within a minute she was steaming round the curve, her exhaust spreading over the Middlebrook valley like a great blanket. What's on it today? *Clan MacDonald* again would get a 'boo', but a 'Scot' or a 'Brit' would bring a cheer. Whatever the outcome, we always went home filled with that same emotion I experience to this day when a steam-hauled

Above: At Lancaster Castle station, No 44709 waits at the signals before continuing on to Barrow-in-Furness.

Below: Waiting at Preston for the train to Wigan, we are rewarded with a view of 'Black Five' No 44902 departing southbound with a fitted freight.

Approaching Euxton Junction, where the line to Chorley, Bolton and Manchester branches off the main line, 8F No 48257, fitted with a snowplough in preparation for work on the high ground in winter, passes us northbound with a train of coal empties, while (*below*) further on we catch up with No 44902 as she too plunges south.

No 44873 takes water for the journey at Preston.

express races by – awe, excitement, something powerful and urgent happening right before your eyes! Happy days…

From Preston, our Class 4 diesel takes us on to Wigan North Western, a trip that proves fruitless, however, as we soon learn that track repairs have forced a diversion about 2 miles south of the station, rejoining the main line a further 5 miles to the north, with only stopping trains being allowed through.

A much-delayed London-Barrow train, Brush-diesel-hauled, takes us back to Preston, from where a Lake District train hauled by 'Black Five' No 44873 will speed us on to Lancaster again.

Soon we are away again, speeding up the WCML for Lancaster, and lucky enough to get the window directly behind the tender of No 44873.

It's bad luck again at Lancaster, though, where we find

From the carriage behind No 44873 we catch a fleeting glimpse of sister engine No 45245 with a passenger train near Brock.

that we will have a long wait before another steam-hauled service can return us to Preston. Feeling rather cheated, we are forced to set off homeward on a diesel multiple unit, so the day ends as it had started – but a memorable steam day none the less!

Meanwhile it's high time to take another look at happenings down at the shed during August. Long gone are the 9Fs and the tank engines; today the variety is much reduced and the survivors are now 'Black Fives', 8Fs and one or two 5MT 4-6-0s, of which No 73014 is without doubt the pick of the bunch, resplendent in her green livery, which contrasts sharply with the grubby unkempt black of her stablemates. She was given a thorough clean and polish here at Bolton shed some time ago to enable her to haul an enthusiasts' special excursion and the staff have kept her looking proud ever since. Most of the other inmates are in

On 23 August 'Black Five' No 45381 gets up steam, with 8F No 48652 behind.

'Black Five' No 45234 simmers at the shed, with 8F No 48437 in the background, on 23 August 1967.

'Black Five' No 45110 receives some attention alongside 8F No 48425 at Bolton shed on 21 August 1967.

5MT 4-6-0 No 73014 reflects the late afternoon sunshine, while out of shot behind her the scrap line is as full as ever.

pretty shoddy condition, with the notable exceptions of 8F No 48425 and 'Black Five' No 45110, which have also received a clean recently and are now simmering gently in the afternoon sunshine.

Many of Bolton's engines have by now had their shed identity plates removed and the name 'Bolton' painted onto their buffer beams, no doubt to foil the growing number of memorabilia hunters who know that soon all this will be a thing of the past.

No fewer than seven of the last representatives of the BR Standard 2MT 2-6-0s are parked awaiting their final journey. Nos 78007, 78012, 78013, 78014, 78023, 78044 and 78062 make a sad sight indeed, as does 'Black Five' No 45304, similarly bereft of connecting rods and piston rods, while gaining rust and losing what paint they still have.

Two days later, and it seems I spoke too soon about No 73014.

The sight I had dreaded: No 73014, 'the pride of Bolton sheds', prematurely consigned to the scrap line with a cracked boiler. It can be seen from the loving shine applied to her paintwork that she is in very good external condition, but now she stands with other locos, condemned to the cutter's torch.

End of the line: BR Standard 2MT No 78013 stands on the scrap line at Bolton shed, with sister engine 78023 behind, on 23 August 1967.

Another visit to the shed, and I can't believe my eyes! There on the scrap line – shining in the dying light – is 73014. It must be some kind of mistake. She looks so good, and she is booked to haul a special rail tour in October.

I ask a passing driver, 'Is she really being scrapped?'

'Yes, I'm afraid so. She has a cracked boiler.'

What a sad end for the pride of the shed.

'They'll all be gone soon,' the gloomy railwayman continues. 'They're closing the shed on 8 June next year.'

How long had I dreaded hearing those words? I shudder at the thought of Bolton's name being added to the ever-increasing list of engine sheds that are being closed and pulled down. The image is alien to me, but for those like the gloomy engineman, who live and work with these great steaming giants every day of their lives, it must be unbearable. I reflect on the feeling of impending doom that has slowly but surely pervaded the buildings in recent times. When did I last see a smiling face here? I doubt I ever will again.

How it was...

On a recent visit to Wigan North Western station I am reminded of how much the steam scene has changed in just a few years. Talking with a fellow enthusiast on the platform, he describes how he has been photographing steam locomotives for over 20 years and has with him a sample of his work, about 300 in all, and suggests that he has enough undeveloped rolls of film at home to keep him busy throughout the winter months.

Looking through the prints he is offering for sale, I notice he has photos of every 'Britannia' locomotive, every 'Duchess', 'Patriot', 'Princess' and most of the 'Royal Scots' and 'Jubilees'. He also has many examples from other railway regions, including several 'A4' and 'A1' 'Pacifics', 'Kings', 'Castles' and 'Battle of Britain'/'West Country' Classes. He is selling his work at a price of 9d each and I am tempted to buy some to keep for posterity. What it does emphasise is just how much more varied and exciting those days were for the railway enthusiast. Today, only the 'Britannias' survive to represent the 'Pacific' classes, with 9Fs and 8Fs taking the heavy-duty work.

The first 'Duchess' 'Pacific' I ever saw was at Preston in 1960. I was making my way towards the engine sheds with some friends, when someone called out that a 'Duchess' was in the station. Scrambling up onto a lorry trailer, which had been conveniently parked by a wall overlooking the station, stretching and straining to see over the wall, there she was! No 46252 *City of Leicester* – what a sight! Steam power at its most impressive, thundering out of the station, its 6ft 9in driving wheels dwarfing a group of workmen on the nearby track. I struggled desperately to keep a grip on the wall, unable to tear my eyes away from the scene as she swept regally past and disappeared behind the sheds. I had to see more…

Wigan was a more cost-effective option for main-line steam for me as a 12-year-old schoolboy, since the fare to Preston or Crewe was seldom within my means. Seen from Wallgate station, locomotives and their trains on the main line out of North Western would be silhouetted. What an unforgettable sight a 'Pacific', in the hands of an enthusiastic crew, could make against the afternoon sky. Crewe station also provided an excellent venue for the enthusiast, especially the long platform that protruded in the direction of the legendary Crewe North shed, home to so many great engines, but which was guarded as though they contained the Crown Jewels! I often stood on the rain-drenched platform, listening with envy and some admiration to those lucky ones who somehow had managed to infiltrate that special place undetected. They told of 'Duchesses', 'Princess' Class 'Pacifics', 'Royal Scots' and 'Jubilees'. All these seemed just a hundred agonising yards out of sight.

One footbridge led from the platform across the lines to the back of the sheds. If you could get across this you were half way there! Then you must sneak along the side of the building past the offices, which seemed to house just about everyone whose role in life seemed to be to prevent access to the prize within. Onwards now past a row of shining Brush-Sulzer diesels, which aroused about as much interest as a DMU would today, then, to complete the mission, step stealthily in through the front entrance of the depot. Now, having gained the inner sanctum, frantically scribble down as many numbers as possible before you're detected and escorted back to the platform again. Returning in triumph, the eager questions begin, each in his turn trying to decide if an attempt on the stronghold would be worthwhile.

Try as I might, and I did, I was never able to complete sightings of all 38 members of the exalted 'Coronation' Class, or 'Duchesses' as they were popularly known. By the end of their lives I still needed three to complete this branch of the nobility – Nos 46224 *Princess Alexandra*, 46239 *City of Chester* and 46256 *Sir William A. Stanier FRS* – but at Crewe there was always the chance that something out of the ordinary might turn up. Western Region locos up from Shrewsbury were just the thing to raise interest levels now and again, and one such honoured us with an appearance. No 6825 *Llanvair Grange* was something of a novelty and attracted much attention for a while, but it became obvious where loyalties lay when a 'Duchess' or 'Princess' came thundering in, dwarfing the Western Region stranger, for the Stanier 'Pacifics' were always firm favourites with the enthusiasts on the West Coast route.

So much for memories – now back to the present day and the dwindling ranks of the survivors…

The 'Belfast Boat Express'

It's time, we decide, to travel up to Preston on the 'Belfast Boat Express', something that I have long wanted to do. This train comes up from Manchester to make its first stop at Bolton. With just one more stop before Preston, at Chorley, it then continues to meet the boat for Belfast at Heysham Harbour, stopping again at Lancaster and Morecambe on the way.

On Friday 25 August 1967 we arrive at Bolton Trinity Street station at 9.15pm to find that the train has arrived early and is already waiting to be on its way once more, hauled by 'Black Five' No 44709, looking in fine form. At 9.20pm the red light from the semaphore signal at the western end of the platform turns to green and we are away, thundering out of the station amid clouds of smoke and with sparks flying high from the chimney, onto the through line to avoid a DMU waiting at the end of the platform, and in no time at all we are racing out of Bolton along the wide valley of the Middlebrook towards Lostock Junction. The bright glow from the cab reflects on our plume of smoke as we accelerate towards the junction, then, at about 50mph, steam is cut off and we cruise through the small station just 5 minutes into our journey.

With effortless ease the 'Black Five' picks up the pace again, speeding through the fading light towards our first stop at Chorley at 9.35pm. Here we pause briefly. Safety valves blow off, deafeningly loud through the open windows just behind the tender. The driver looks back with anxious glances at his watch. He is impatient to be away. The green light shows at 9.40pm and with fantastic acceleration we execute another remarkable get-away. Thundering along at a tremendous pace, sparks fly and from the open windows of the leading coach we feel the warm glow of the raging fire in the cab. Now, head out of the window, conscious only of smoke, steam and heat, we plunge onwards to the main line.

Euxton Junction approaches and we slow to join the West Coast route, but with green lights proclaiming the way to the horizon we are soon picking up the pace and speed through Leyland at 9.37pm, ahead of time! Not far from Preston now, and an amber light forces us to slow to about 20mph for our approach. We pass 'Britannia' No 70032 *Tennyson* as she gives way to let us through, before she too can enter the station with her parcels train.

At 9.55pm we come to a halt at Preston station. Sister engine No 45436 is waiting to leave with a southbound freight as we disembark, still exhilarated, and make for the northern end of the platform. No 44709 takes on water to quench her thirst before continuing her journey. She's on time, but must now follow the 'Ulster Express', hauled by a 'Brush 4' diesel, holding up proceedings for our impatient crew.

At 10.07pm at last the 'Belfast Boat Express' gets the green light. A spirited departure takes her on her way up to Heysham Harbour and the waiting ferry to Ireland, just as 'Brit 32', *Tennyson*, pulls in with her train. We wander over for a word with her driver. He talks fondly of the times when he was a fireman, working on the 'Duchess' 'Pacifics' in their heyday, and recalls with enthusiasm how once they had reached 120mph as a result of his shovelling.

'Never managed that yet with a diesel,' he says, and is clearly happy to be given these last opportunities to coax the best from this ageing fleet. He goes on to describe the ease with which the 'Duchesses' could be fired, compared to the 'Britannias', which at best, he says, require a lot of effort for a poor result.

It's now 10.37pm and time for farewells as *Tennyson* gets the green light. A quick 'Goodbye lads' from the driver, a couple of shrill whistles and they are off, billowing clouds of smoke and escaping steam, onwards towards Shap and Carlisle. For us, shelter for the night is called for. The waiting rooms on the main-line platforms are full of dozing bodies, so we make our way across the station to find alternatives. We are in luck. The branch-line waiting rooms are almost empty, so we pull the cords to fire up the ceiling heaters for a while, and settle down for the night. It's been a great evening – what will the morning bring? We would find out soon enough, and what a treat was in store...

We decide to take this opportunity of a ride up to Lancaster – and what a ride it turns out to be, as the accompanying photographs show.

As our last sight of the day at Preston, clean and tidy 'Britannia' No 70014 *Iron Duke*, heads south, we prepare for our homeward journey, a fitting end to a tremendous steam day – 'Britannias' in abundance and 'Black Fives' everywhere, and at least some of them in presentable condition. Someone in the sheds still cares!

Above: The first of an impressive list of 'Britannia' locomotives seen on that Saturday, 26 August 1967, is No 70010 *Owen Glendower*, in very grimy condition at Preston with a northbound special passenger train. Interestingly, the names written on her smoke deflectors are in English on one side and in Welsh – *Owain Glendwyr* – on the other.

Below: Owen Glendower prepares to leave Preston.

On board, we pass 'Black Five' No 45349 as she sidles past the spot where Preston sheds (24K) used to stand, marked now only by rows of rusty rails.

Above: After a terrific sprint up to Lancaster, No 70010 continues northwards and we wait to see what will take out return trip to Preston.

Below: Shortly after the spirited departure of *Owen Glendower*, an equally spirited arrival in the form of smartly turned-out 'Black Five' No 45227.

Above: Safety valves still blowing off, No 45227 departs from Lancaster Castle station for the north.

Below: Closely following the departure of No 45227, sister engine No 44780 appears. Rather grubby, and held at the signal with her parcels train, she waits her turn to follow northwards.

Above: The last steam-hauled train through Lancaster before our departure for Preston is a southbound petroleum tanker train hauled by 'Britannia' No 70024 Vulcan, seen here held at signals by the box. Her crew appear keen to get into the picture.

Below: The driver and fireman are keen to be recorded for posterity as No 70024 Gets the all clear to continue her southward journey.

Above: Back at Preston after an unremarkable trip behind an E-E Type 4, No 70024 arrives and passes through the station while 'Black Five' No 44727 fills the canopy with steam from her safety valves as her fireman attends to her oil lamps. No 44727 was built in 1949 and was one of only ten experimental locos, in a class numbering over 840, to be fitted with a steel firebox.

Below: On what is developing into a tremendous steam day, 'Britannia' No 70012 *John of Gaunt* pauses to take on water before departing northwards with her fitted freight train.

Above: Moments later, No 70012 storms out from beneath the bridge to the north of Preston's platforms with her freight train.

Below: *John of Gaunt*'s driver looks back as she passes the dumpy signals and Preston's northerly signal box.

Stanier 'Black Five' No 45421 takes water at the northern end of Preston station before continuing her journey. The loco is carrying both the shed code plate (10D) on her smokebox door and the name of her home shed (Lostock Hall) on her buffer beam. Most engines carry either shed plate or name – few have both, and many have neither these days.

Above: It's turning into a great day for 'Britannias', as No 70022 *Tornado* departs from Preston with a parcels train for Crewe and the south. I wonder how long these old workhorses have left now…

Below: Scruffy 'Britannia' No 70035 *Rudyard Kipling* hurries north through Preston with a fitted freight train.

Above: In contrast to *Rudyard Kipling*, 'Black Five' No 45000 looks smart as she speeds through Preston with a non-stop passenger train. Rumour has it that she is scheduled for preservation, and certainly appears to merit it after her clean-up at her home shed, Lostock Hall.

Below: Stanier Class 5 No 45130 enters Preston station with a passenger train from the south.

A beautiful sight as 'Britannia' No 70014 *Iron Duke* appears to be in superb condition with polished green boiler and tender, shiny red buffer beam, clean numbers and legible name. A sight worth waiting for!

As No 70014 departs from Preston for the south, amid shrill whistles and pillars of steam from her safety valves, it's almost time for us to be making our way home as well.

Then a couple of pleasant final surprises, as if the day could get any better. Our train home turns out to be steam-hauled in the shape of 'Black Five' No 44861 pulling a Barrow-Manchester express. And another treat – and as we leave, a final 'Britannia' completes the tally of nine for the day, as No 70004 *William Shakespeare* rolls into the platform, tired-looking and grimy, hauling a fitted freight train. A lively run home ends a perfect day on the West Coast Main Line.

• • •

With the sight of steam-hauled expresses becoming rarer day by day, especially when away from the main line, I find it increasingly hard to let a night go by without watching the 'Belfast Boat Express', either as it thunders out of Trinity Street's platform, or roars through the shell of Lostock Junction's closed station. Motive power for this popular train can vary with availability and so, inevitably, can performances. The regular engine that did so well on this run, 'Black Five' No 45435, has not been seen for some time now, being more than adequately replaced by No 44709.

Many evenings I climb into my friend's van and we race from Bolton to Lostock Junction, arriving to see the lights green in anticipation. 9.20pm. Any moment now! A few long minutes pass, but the sound of powerful exhaust beats heralds the shattering of the quietness in that still rural setting. Sparks fly, smoke trails from the racing engine and the smells of steam power fill the night air. As quickly as it is upon us, so it is gone. Signals return to danger and we return to the world of the internal combustion engine, treasuring another encounter in the diminishing world of steam on our railways.

• • •

Reading through the current editions of railway magazines brings home the reality of the demise of steam on our railways. In 1962, only five years ago, the withdrawal of steam locomotives was gathering pace: 'Patriots' and 'Princesses' from the LMR, 'Halls', 'Castles' and 'Kings' from the WR, 'B1s' and 'V2s' from the ER, and the first of the 'WD' 2-8-0s, including Nos 90060, 90244, 90248, 90436, 90505 and 90616. This really was the beginning of the end. The process continued and the pace of withdrawals increased through the years as more and more steam locos were scrapped. No class of engines was immune, no region exempt, but for me it was the demise across the network of the once great 'Pacific' classes that hurt the most, so that now, in 1967, only the 'Britannia' 'Pacifics' remain in numbers.

It's now the end of August 1967 and the pattern of withdrawals continues. Most of the 'A4s' have gone – recent casualties include Nos 60024 *Kingfisher* and 60034 *Lord Faringdon*. The majority of the remaining 'Jubilees' and 'WD' 2-8-0s shedded at Leeds and Wakefield have also been scrapped, together with some of the last of the 'B1s'. On the London Midland Region, vigorous withdrawals of the surviving 'Black Fives' and 8Fs is evident, together with a whole clutch of the mighty 9F 2-10-0s, including Nos 92006/18/30/32/65/74/76/83/87/89/96/104/107/150 and 151. Hand in hand with this wholesale scrapping comes news of further shed closures in the region, with Skipton (10G) being one of the notable losses.

On the Southern Region the last 'Pacifics' were scrapped between Easter and June of this year and there is now very little steam working in the region, with the exception of one or two tank engines and 'Standard 5s' doing occasional freight work. Most of the surviving SR steam locos were withdrawn before Easter, including 2-6-4 tanks Nos 80012 and 80019, together with 'Standard 5s' Nos 73002, 73115/17 and 19, and what are probably the last of the 'West Country' and 'Battle of Britain' locos, Nos 34006 *Bude*, 34019 *Bideford* and 34088 *213 Squadron*.

On the Western Region hardly anything is left. Their quota of 2-6-2 and 2-6-4 tanks have nearly all gone, as have their 'Standard 5s', many of which carried names, such as No 73086 *The Green Knight*, which following withdrawal was ignominiously towed away from Westbury on 22 January by 'Warship' No D844 *Spartan*.

And finally, on the Scottish Region the story is much the same as elsewhere, with main-line traffic being virtually all diesel-hauled, with but a tiny handful of steam locos still in service. These are mostly 2-6-4 tanks such as Nos 80116 and 80120, which are used as pilot engines, and one or two 'Black Fives', including Nos 45359 and 45423, which have been reprieved at Motherwell motive power depot and fitted with snowploughs.

But sightings of steam engines are dwindling fast. Only on the LMR can steam still be seen on passenger trains, with the greatest concentration being around the Preston area. I know, though, that this is only a stay of execution, as I read of the recent demise of 'Britannias' Nos 70027 *Rising Star*, 70033 *Charles Dickens*, 70040 *Clive of India*, 70041 *Sir John Moore*, 70046 *Anzac*, 70052 *Firth of Tay* and 70053 *Moray Firth*. Sad reading indeed, but when coupled with the fact that every month sees more 'Black Fives', 8Fs, 'Standard 5s' and 9Fs being cut up, it becomes painfully obvious that the end is near. So I can do no more than spend these last few months of steam engine history recording the images of what precious few remain and continue to give so much pleasure to the hundreds of enthusiasts still thronging the West Coast Main Line.

Of course, we are now in the blossoming era of the steam

'Britannia' No 70031 *Byron* takes on water at Bolton Trinity Street station before continuing with her parcels train towards Manchester. Note the imposing structure of the London Midland & Scottish Railway goods warehouse behind.

locomotive preservation societies, visionaries who see it as their calling to save that which BR has doomed. Closed branch lines are being bought up and money raised for re-opening, while 'enthusiast specials', steam-hauled excursions, are regularly being organised. Perhaps steam will indeed live on?

• • •

It's Bank Holiday Monday, 28 August, and an ideal opportunity to take a ride up to Preston in the hope that extra trains might be provided, and that they might be steam-hauled.

The day starts well. On our arrival at Bolton Trinity Street station we are greeted with the sight of 'Britannia' No 70031 *Byron*, waiting to take an eastbound parcels train.

Though we leave Trinity Street station with high hopes, reality does not meet expectation. 'Specials' are few and far between, and diesel-hauled into the bargain. Our other hope, goods traffic, often steam-hauled now, has been suspended because of the holiday traffic. Our only sight of a steam loco at Preston turns out to be a 'Black Five' travelling light engine through the station. Total disappointment! We take a train back to Bolton in the hope of spending some time at the sheds, but late-running trains mean that by the time we arrive there the light has deserted us for the day, so what started so promisingly ends gloomily, in every sense.

SEPTEMBER

It's Friday night, or should I say Saturday morning, 2 September 1967. It's Preston station, 2.30am, and I'm aboard a sleeping car express bound for Glasgow and Edinburgh. My destination, together with a couple of enthusiast friends, is Carlisle, and we depart 3 minutes late at 2.38am. This being my first trip over Shap, my intention is 1) to stay awake and 2) to log the journey for comparison with steam runs a decade earlier.

We leave as 'Britannia' No 70032 *Tennyson* is arriving with a train for Barrow. Our train, with Brush Type 4 No D1625 in charge, is hauling 15 coaches, mostly heavy sleeping cars, giving a full weight of about 600 tons. We get off to a healthy start and pass Lancaster at 3.01am, in spite of yellow lights outside Preston, and are checked again at Morecambe South Junction, but then our driver gets the green light and responds smartly to get us racing northwards again, soon covering the 9 miles to Hest Bank and roaring through Carnforth at 3.12am.

By Oxenholme, nearly 20 miles out of Lancaster, the time is 3.22am and the typical Pennine drizzle gets heavier as we round the curves, green lights reflecting from the wet tracks. As we approach Grayrigg Summit, north of Oxenholme, we get a taste of things to come, as our speed starts to fall steadily, then picks up down to Tebay, only to be checked again to near 10mph near Dillicar signal box. Once clear of Tebay we accelerate smartly for our assault on Shap Summit, and as we climb the lower reaches of the incline our engine noise gets noticeably louder as our speed drops again. We climb higher, engine roaring threateningly, throwing exhaust fumes high into the heavy drizzle as our speed falls

77

further, until we clear the summit travelling at about 35mph and pass Shap station at 3.50am. The distance from Lancaster of 39.7 miles is covered in 49 minutes. Not bad considering the signal checks, but, to put it into perspective, 'Coronation' Class No 46228 *Duchess of Rutland* was clocked to here in 49.5 minutes with a similar load on the 'Mid-day Scot', while 'Princess' Class No 46206 *Princess Marie Louise* put them both to shame with a time of 38 minutes pulling the same train.

We are now accelerating down the long descent to Penrith, passed at 4.00am, only to be brought to a complete stop at the north of the station for about 5 minutes. When we get away again, we take the remainder of the journey at a leisurely pace and come to a halt at Carlisle Citadel at 4.25am, having covered the 81 miles from Preston in 107 minutes, for an average speed of 49mph. Taking into consideration our heavy load, poor weather and four speed checks, this is a creditable performance, but bettered by both the 'Duchess' and the 'Princess', with average speeds of 55.2 and 53mph respectively!

Carlisle station is dark and draughty, yet unusually peaceful, the silence broken only by the occasional piercing whistle of 'Britannia' No 70012 *John of Gaunt* as she waits to take the main line with a southbound parcels train. We take the opportunity of grabbing a couple of hours' sleep in the waiting room before the next train back leaves for Carnforth at 6.40am. This turns out to be a DMU, which rattles its way towards Shap as I drift in and out of sleep. A brief stop at Shap station wakens me and brings back memories of our visit in June of last year, when we had chatted with the Station Master, who, spending much of his time in his own company, relished the opportunity to talk about his job and the changes he had seen while employed in this lovely yet remote part of the system. Sleep returns until our train pulls

Above: Stanier 'Black Five' No 44917 waits at the northern end of Preston station on Saturday 2 September 1967 with the 14:15 to Barrow, running 15 minutes late.

Below: The train gets away behind Brush diesel No D1954. This month will almost certainly see the end of regular steam-hauled passenger services, but steam on goods will hopefully remain with us until mid-1968.

At the south of Preston station 'Black Five' No 45436 waits as parcels are loaded, and takes the opportunity to top up with water, as nowadays there are no water troughs remaining, where this could be done en route.

Above: Later, within the darker confines of the station platforms, a passenger train hauled by sister engine No 45411 comes to a halt amid clouds of steam.

Below: 'Black Five' No 45450 of Lostock Hall waits to take the rear portion of the passenger train left by the previous engine, as I take a ride up to Lancaster and take this departing shot from my carriage window.

81

Above: Back at Preston, the highlight of the day! 'Britannia' No 70032 *Tennyson* arrives from the north with an express passenger train.

Below: A northbound special eases into Preston from the south to bring another day's 'steaming' to a close. 'Black Five' No 45131 runs under the signal gantry.

into Carnforth, where we have a short wait before our connection to Preston appears in the form of an English Electric Type 4. As diesels go, these are fine engines, arguably inferior only to the 'Deltics', so we settle down in preparation for a well-earned breakfast and the prospect of another good day's steaming, camera and notebook at the ready.

With the end of August comes the end of many of the Saturdays-only summer season excursions that regularly feature steam locos, and today is probably their last full day, with a run-down to 16 September, when any remaining steam on 'SOs' will be terminated, though some steam haulage will remain, notably on goods trains. The contrast between last week and today is immediately noticeable, as we see only three 'Britannias' compared with nine last Saturday, though 'Black Fives' continue to provide plenty of interest.

More bad news

September magazines bring more bad news. Withdrawals coming to light at the beginning of September 1967 are many and varied, as has so often been the case in recent months. The Southern Region, which officially saw its last steam-hauled passenger services on the weekend of 8/9 July, is probably the hardest hit, losing a further 26 'BB/WC' Class locos and seven more from the 'Merchant Navy' Class. These may well represent the last of the SR 'Pacifics'. The fact that no further withdrawals are notified for the WR could mean that steam is now extinct in this region, almost five years to the month since the first 'Halls', 'Castles' and 'Kings' were withdrawn.

On the LMR the steam population continues to be depleted, with the loss of a further 120 locos, including 24

Stanier 'Black Fives', 22 8Fs, 12 'Standard 5s', 14 of the last BR Standard Class 3 and Class 4 tank engines (number series 80xxx and 82xxx) and five of the remaining 9F 2-10-0s. On the ER little steam is left, a sorry state of affairs witnessed by the listing of only one withdrawn locomotive, Class 2F 0-6-0 No 65345, introduced as long ago as 1888 and of North British Railway design.

Motive power depot changes announced recently also make dismal reading and include Aintree (8L), closed on 12 June, Sutton Oak (8G), 9 June, and Nine Elms (70A), Guildford (70C), Salisbury (70E) and Weymouth (70G) on 9 July. Although steam power is still prominent between Crewe and Carlisle, the amount of steam working out of Crewe South shed is gradually declining and the depot is expected to be closed to steam in November 1967. With the summer of 1967 coming to an end and thoughts turning to winter, it seems that the unstoppable demise of steam on our railways is accelerating towards its inevitable conclusion. This will certainly be the last winter that the vast majority of our well-loved locos will ever see.

Saturday 16 September brings another trip up to Preston. Today is the day designated for the termination of the majority of the Saturdays-only specials of the summer holiday season, although many were taken off on 2 and 9 September. I travel with high expectations. As it turns out it is a pretty poor day by recent standards.

Only one 'Britannia' graces the station, No 70021 *Morning Star*, on a parcels train. Most of the Manchester trains are off because of a rail strike by guards, so services such as the Manchester-Barrow, a regular steam working, are noticeably absent. In addition, an enthusiasts' excursion due to be hauled by one of Leeds Holbeck's two remaining 'Jubilees' is also cancelled because of the rail dispute, as is another special scheduled for preserved 'A3' *Flying Scotsman*,

Above: Only one steam-hauled passenger train puts in an appearance, a London to Barrow-in-Furness service, hauled not by the usual 'Britannia', but by 'Black Five' No 45209, seen leaving Preston.

Below: 9F No 92009 leaves Preston with a northbound freight on the morning of 16 September, one of the few steam-hauled trains of the day.

Above: Stanier 'Black Fives' are by far the most numerous of the remaining steam locomotives in the country. Here, No 45279 is seen waiting to leave Preston with a northbound parcels train on the same day.

Below and opposite: The only 'Britannia' representative on 16 September, No 70021 *Morning Star*, is well worth waiting for. Seen first emerging from the shadows of the platforms, then leaving Preston with her southbound parcels train, she still sports her 12A Carlisle Kingmoor shed plate, and is my last sight of steam for another day.

After the 'Black Fives', Stanier 8Fs account for a large proportion of the 'rest'. No 48631 is seen leaving Preston later the same day with a soda-ash train for the north.

which was due to run through Bolton en route for Morecambe tomorrow morning. So all in all a disappointing day both in terms of news and views, and already it is evident that there are markedly fewer steam-hauled trains than there were even a month ago. It is a hard fact that soon there will be none at all.

On Tuesday 19 September I visit Bolton shed, which on this occasion seems to be housing fewer engines than usual. A quick count suggests about 30 in all, consisting largely of Stanier 'Black Fives' and 8Fs, with one or two 'Standard 5s', some of which look to be in pretty run-down condition. Standing out, though, and showing evidence of preparation for enthusiasts' special excursions booked for the near future, are 'Black Five' No 45110 and 5MT No 73040. Both look well oiled and slick after receiving the attentions of some diligent railwaymen. Shame about the rest. The scrap lines are full, as usual now, the only new addition being 8F No 48106.

Extra room has been set aside within the shed buildings for the latest condemned inmates. Here I find BR Class 5 No 73070 and 8F No 48417 waiting to be towed away and cut up for scrap, their final destination having been chalked on their grimy tenders: 'J. Cashmore Ltd, Great Bridge, Staffs'.

OCTOBER

On Wednesday 4 October 1967 I'm on my way to the sheds again, walking from Trinity Street station past Orlando Bridge, when steam engine whistles direct me onto the footbridge by Bolton East signal box. Here I see the driver of 'Black Five' No 45347 getting restless as he is having to wait for his signal to be pulled off, which can't happen until the signalman in Bolton East box can get sister engine No 45415 out of the way to clear the road towards Manchester for the parcels train. Eventually the light engine is shifted towards the station, allowing No 45347 to get on with her job, and peace returns to Orlando Bridge.

Arriving at the sheds after the brief excitement at Orlando Bridge, I am disappointed to find only about a dozen engines in, though I shouldn't be surprised as it's late afternoon and even the last of Bolton's ageing fleet have to earn their keep. Three newcomers have appeared on the scrap line, 'Standard 5' No 73048, and two 'Black Fives', Nos 44866 and 44927. The coupling and piston rods are already missing from 44866, but 44927 seems still intact. To see so many engines still in working order and awaiting the scrap-man here today is truly a sad sight. I watch as Drewry 0-6-0 shunter No D2234 (introduced in 1955) trundles away, and turn my camera to 'Standard 5' No 73048, introduced in 1951 and thus only four years older, yet those four years of hard labour have reduced the steam loco to a heap of scrap. I wonder how long the diesel shunter will survive.

Time to head for home again, but on the way I can't resist another stop at Orlando Bridge, where I spent so much time when younger. In a final 5 minutes in the dim light of the late

'Black Five' No 45415 runs light engine towards Bolton Trinity Street station, allowing sister engine No 45347 to speed her parcels train past Bolton East signal box towards Manchester.

Above: 'Standard 5' No 73069 waits at the entrance to part of Bolton sheds for her next duty. In the darkness of the shed 'Black Five' No 45377 can just be seen.

Below: On the scrap line, 'Standard 5' No 73048 waits tender-to-tender with 'Black Five' No 44866.

afternoon of an October day, through the gloom the steam locos work on. I can make out 'Standard 5' No 73040 with her newly painted smokebox door and number plate, looking splendid on a fairly menial duty hauling a load of old railway sleepers towards the west. 'Black Five' No 45375 drags an electric multiple unit of the M29xxxM series. I wonder if the steam crew smile ironically to each other? An unidentifiable 8F waits to depart towards Bury with her goods train, while another 8F in the sidings towards Burnden Junction and the sheds simmers quietly. Next comes 'Black Five' No 45415, the cause of the hold-up earlier in the afternoon, now at the head of an eastbound parcels train herself and speeding on her way past Bolton East box. It's only been a few minutes, yet steam workings have occupied centre-stage throughout, bringing back happy memories. Only three classes represented now. In years gone by there would have been so many.

On my way home I buy this month's editions of the railway magazines and wonder what further bad news they will bring me. As expected, bad news there is, in plenty. Withdrawals listed in the October magazines are mainly from the LMR, which number about 140 locomotives for the month. Classes involved (with totals withdrawn in brackets) are: 2-6-4 tanks (11); Stanier 'Black Fives' (24); 8F 2-8-0s (15); Standard Class 5 4-6-0s (15 – notably including our 'favourite', No 73014); ex-WD 2-8-0s (52 – most of which had been operating on Scottish Region metals); and 9F 2-10-0s (14). In addition to these 'workhorses', 'named-engine' classes also suffer more losses, including one of the last 'Jubilees', No 45675 *Hardy* (which probably leaves No 45697 *Achilles* as the only surviving member of the class, apart from those scheduled for preservation, which as far as I am aware are Nos 45593 *Kholapur* and 45596 *Bahamas*). Four more of the remaining 'Britannias' have also gone, namely Nos 70005 *John Milton*, 70015 *Apollo*, 70038 *Robin Hood* and the un-named 70047. The withdrawal of *Robin Hood* is the major shock, after seeing her recently in apparently good condition at Preston.

On the ER withdrawals total just over 30 and include six of the remaining 'B1s', ten of the last of the 'J27' 0-6-0s and a handful of 'Austerity' 2-8-0s. Another steam shed was served with closure recently, as Stoke-on-Trent (5D) was closed to steam on and from 7 August. The magazines note that steam power continues prominently north of Crewe, Manchester and Liverpool on West Coast Main Line summer-Saturday traffic, and there were at least ten steam passenger trains through Preston on weekdays in the summer, consisting mainly of Stanier Class 5 4-6-0s and interspersed 'Britannia' workings. But it is noted that with the summer season now at an end, this state of affairs cannot be expected to continue. The November edition of *Railway World* contains a paragraph of particular relevance to the current position of steam on the railways:

'The North Western lines of the LM will be the last areas to have steam haulage on BR, with sheds in the Manchester area scheduled as the last to lose steam traction. The present programme of shed closures to steam traction is now: November, Crewe South and Birkenhead; December, Springs Branch; January 1968, Carlisle area including Kingmore, Workington and Tebay; March, Northwich, Trafford Park and Buxton; May, Speke Junction, Edge Hill, Stockport and Heaton Mersey; and August, Patricroft, Lostock Hall, Bolton, Newton Heath, Carnforth and Rose Grove.'

This will be the end of steam. Part of the final change-over from steam to diesel traction will be covered by the latest deliveries of new Type 1 and Type 2 locomotives, partly by drafting in redundant diesel locomotives from other regions and partly by the delivery of new E-E Type 4s at present under construction (D400-49). Almost all the withdrawals that came to light this month are of LM engines, with a handful of the last steam survivors from the ER. In fact, steam traction came to an end in North East England at the beginning of September, and a main article in *Railway World* this month is entitled 'End of steam in the North East', which follows another similar article in September's issue entitled 'Steam's last fling on the Southern'. How long will it be before we read 'Farewell to steam on the LMR'? A sad thought.

NOVEMBER

On Thursday evening, 9 November 1967, I decide it's about time to renew acquaintance with Trinity Street station and the Manchester-Heysham Harbour express. For over a week now the boat train has been in the hands of E-E Type 4 diesels, but a friend has seen the train on Wednesday and reported steam to be reinstated at its head. I arrive at 9.15pm to find the train already waiting at the platform, with Stanier 'Black Five' No 45435 back in charge. This was the first loco I saw on this run and she has not been at its head for some time, but tonight she's had a clean and polish and looks in fine condition, as I stand alongside and watch her fireman putting finishing touches to her fire in preparation for the off. Thick black smoke is already belching from her chimney into the cold night air.

Soon the green light is given and No 45435 thunders into action, disappearing round the curve and already picking up the pace towards Chorley and the West Coast Main Line, when, to our surprise, we notice that another steam-hauled train has quietly made its way into the station, a short parcels train hauled by Bolton shed's own 'Standard 5' No 73069, which has also had a clean and looks resplendent with newly painted bright red buffer beam. The warmth of her fire is very welcome on this cold night, but regrettably short-lived, as soon she too is off into the darkness in the direction of the sheds, leaving me to shiver on the platform, but glad to be still able to see steam at work here in Bolton.

On Saturday 18 November I go up to Preston again for the first time in some weeks. I arrive at Trinity Street station at 9.30am to find the next available train is at 10.00am. So we wait and soon the quiet of the morning is shattered by the thunder of two Stanier 8Fs working in unison, double-heading a long and very heavy train of new track. Nos 48386 and 48369 heave their weighty load through the station towards Chorley and the main line beyond, amid vast clouds of smoke and steam. Slowly they disappear, but the volume of their exhausts can still be heard long after the last of their load is out of sight.

Our train is a DMU. We climb aboard and head for Chorley. Soon we are held at signals, as the twin 8Fs are directed out of the way, and as we wait we in turn are passed by Stanier 'Black Five' No 45310 hurrying by with her freight train. Now we get the signal and hurry past the 8Fs and on towards Euxton Junction to join the West Coast Main Line, where another 8F, No 48510, is being held up to allow us to proceed at speed. Approaching Preston at 10.30am, we pass 'Britannia' No 70012 *John of Gaunt* as she waits to enter the station., while 8F No 48646 pauses before taking her freight southwards. At 11.00am *John of Gaunt* makes her spectacular entrance, safety valves blowing off and steam and smoke shooting high into the cold blue sky, while the sun glints on the still frost-covered tracks. Repeated whistles sound as the driver shows his impatience at being held up again at signals, and soon a crowd gathers around the locomotive to witness a spirited departure as her regulator is opened. Wheels spin on frosty tracks, steam screams from safety valves and yet more whistles fill the air, as the 'Britannia' and her crew head for the open road at last.

Preston station returns to calm, but only briefly, as 11.30am brings a deluge of steam activity. First into the station comes 'Black Five' No 45017, the loco currently working the 'Belfast Boat Express'. A Carnforth engine, she really is in first-class condition. Next, the two 8Fs arrive, still working hard and much appreciated by enthusiasts and ordinary passengers alike as they heave their massive load through the station. Simultaneously, 'Black Five' No 44831 arrives with a southbound parcels train. She takes water as her relief driver and fireman arrive. The crews exchange greetings, and the new men are pleased to hear, 'She's in good nick.'

'For how long?' I think to myself.

At 11.45am I see my first blue E-E Type 4, No D245. Later in the day I see my second, D248. Thankfully, steam soon returns in the form of 'Britannia' No 70024 *Vulcan*, which emerges from the south, working hard at the head of a heavy coal train, filling the platform with smoke, at about 12.00 noon. Leaving Preston at 12.24pm aboard the Manchester portion of a Glasgow-Euston express, which today is steam-hauled by 'Black Five' No 45381 for this part of the journey, rather than the more usual 'Brush 4', we seem to require no effort to make up the lost 10 minutes incurred by a wait at the platform, and trundle into Bolton's Trinity Street station at 12.55pm, just after overtaking sister engine No 44831 seen earlier.

We try again, boarding a DMU for Preston, and from there take a train for Burnley, just by way of a change. I've never been to Burnley before. The highlight of this expedition turns out to be Stanier 8F No 48492, simmering gloomily in the foggy station, on which we now face an hour's wait for a return train to Bolton. Dismal station, freezing fog, crowded DMU back home. Not a great idea!

The December issue of *Railway World* continues the pattern of the steam run-down of previous months, with a sad list of over 200 newly withdrawn locomotives, including over 50 Stanier 'Black Fives' and nearly 30 of the remaining 8Fs, together with eight of the last 9F 2-10-0s. There can't be many of these great machines left now and I've noticed they are conspicuous by their absence up at Preston these days. All but about a dozen of the withdrawn locos are from the LMR and this again reflects the sorry state of steam traction on the network today. The most unhappy loss is that of another four of the remaining 'Britannia' 'Pacifics', Nos 70010 *Owen Glendower* (can this be?), 70028 *Royal Star*, 70032 *Tennyson* and 70039 *Sir Christopher Wren* (the only member of this quartet I haven't photographed). By my reckoning, there can be no more than ten 'Britannia' Class locos left now – it's all very depressing!

Depressing also is the news of the closure of the main-line shed at Warrington (8B), on 2 October. All this reminds me, as if I needed reminding, that this is steam's last winter. The urgency for photographing the last of these mighty beasts grows more pressing day by day.

DECEMBER

On 10 December 1967 a visit is made to Bolton sheds after a very slight fall of snow. There's a dwindling choice of subjects, though the scrap lines are very full, consisting of Stanier 'Black Five' No 45415, 8F Nos 48425, 48436, 48469, 48534 and 48764, and BR Class 5 Nos 73004, 73014 and 73048. Other locos on shed are 'Black Five' Nos 44728, 44866, 44927, 45290, 45318 and 45377; 8F Nos 48166, 48313, 48559 and 48740; and 'Standard 5' No 73156. Of these, Nos 44728, 44866 and 44927 are in store, pending delivery to Cashmore's, as is No 48313. Only Nos 45290 and 48559 are in steam.

Below and right: Stanier locos in store back-to-back: 'Black Five' No 45377 and 8F No 48313.

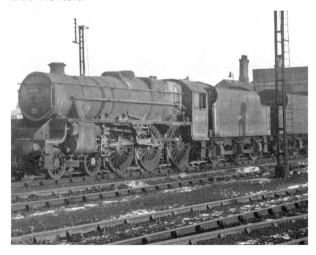

Above: The scrap lines on 10 December 1967: 'Black Fives', 8Fs and 'Standard 5s' await their final journey, with wagons alongside for off-loading their unused coal.

Below: Grimy 8F No 48559 awaits her next call.

1968

JANUARY AND FEBRUARY

The February 1968 edition of *The Railway Magazine* contains more depressing news in the form of an advertisement aimed at preserving a 'Britannia' 'Pacific': 'The scrapping process is gathering momentum and all remaining "Britannias" were withdrawn on 1/1/68.' No 70029 was withdrawn recently, according to the magazine, and the sad loss of No 70031 *Byron* is also reported. Added to this, the list of 9Fs that have gone is growing ever longer – there can't be many left now. Crewe South (5B) and Birkenhead (8H) depots were closed to steam on and from 6 November 1967.

Saturday 3 February 1968 dawns with a dusting of snow. It's been a couple of months since my last visit to Bolton sheds, and I notice immediately on walking through the gates that the previous occupants of the scrap lines are all gone, being replaced by three 8Fs, Nos 48046, 48200 and 48469.

Within the shelter of the sheds proper, a total of 18 locos wait: 'Black Five' Nos 44728, 45294 (in steam), 45425 (marked 'J. Butticiek, Private Sidings, Newport, Mon'), 44715, 45025, 45290, 45377, 44758, 45104, 45318 and 45110 (the last three in steam); BR Class 5 Nos 73069 and 73004 (marked 'J. Cashmore, Town Dock, Newport, Mon'); and 8F Nos 48436, 48380 (in steam), 48764, 48559 and 48773.

8F No 48469 stands alone on the scrap line (*top*), while sister engine No 48046 awaits the same fate. Finally, Nos 48046 and 48200 stand in the snow.

Outside the sheds, BR Class 5 No 73040 stands alone in the snow.

Above: The Standard 4-6-0 is soon joined by returning 8F No 48740, which takes water before seeking refuge from further snow falls, leaving No 73040, seen in the background, alone outside Bolton shed once more.

Below: Back on the WCML on 26 February, sister 8F No 48081 thunders northwards through Preston with a heavy load of coal wagons, and looks in pretty fine condition too!

Stanier 'Black Five' No 45447 waits at the signals before departing from Preston northwards with a coal train.

On Monday 26 February it's time for a long-awaited opportunity to revisit the West Coast Main Line at Preston. Mondays are good days for observing steam workings, as steam locos take charge of goods trains held in abeyance over the weekend.

Steam-hauled passenger services are increasingly rare now, though encouragingly the Manchester-Heysham Harbour 'Belfast Boat Express' is still among those rarities, in both directions. On the evening of 26 February I have the pleasure of witnessing its enthusiastic departure from Bolton Trinity Street station with 'Black Five' No 45134 in charge. Still thrilling!

8F No 48553 steams southwards with her load of empty bogie wagons.

MARCH

Early March 1968 brings more cold weather with occasional snow showers – not the most inviting conditions to venture out with a camera, but the call of steam and the lure of the sheds proves too great an attraction. However, the snowy conditions soon disappear as the March sunshine gets to work.

The March 1968 editions of *Railway World* and *The Railway Magazine* confirm the sad news of last month, that we have seen the last of the 'Pacifics' with the withdrawal of the remaining 'Britannias'. The last to go were Nos 70004 *William Shakespeare*, 70011 *Hotspur*, 70012 *John of Gaunt*, 70014 *Iron Duke*, 70021 *Morning Star*, 70022 *Tornado*, 70023 *Venus*, 70024 *Vulcan*, 70025 *Western Star*, 70035 *Rudyard Kipling*, 70045 *Lord Rowallan*, 70049 *Solway Firth* and 70051 *Firth of Forth*. I can find no words to describe their sad loss.

So few 9F 2-10-0s are left now – only six are listed as withdrawn this month, Nos 92017, 92055, 92110, 92117, 92125 and 92204. Stanier's great workhorses, the 'Black Fives' and 8Fs, account for the majority still in steam on the network, but this month's railway press reports the demise of a further 24 'Black Fives' and 15 8Fs. Other news reported includes the date of Saturday 30 December 1967 as having been the last day for regular steam workings over Shap Summit. Tebay depot was closed to steam from 1 January 1968, its Class 4 4-6-0 bankers being replaced by three Type 1 diesels from that date, to give the heavy trains their much-needed shove up the hill. Springs Branch MPD at Wigan (8F) was closed to steam on and from 4 December.

A footnote to the 'Britannia' situation is that No 70013

Above: Stanier 'Black Five' No 45381 heads the queue under the coaling tower at Bolton shed.

Below: These Stanier 'Black Fives' waiting outside Bolton sheds are Nos 45377 and 45294.

Sister engine No 45260 looks well after being coaled up on a cold but sunny afternoon.

Stanier 8F No 48702 is ready for duty after having been coaled.

Another day and another load of coal for Bolton stalwart, 'Black Five' No 45381.

Oliver Cromwell has been preserved by BR in place of the proposed No 70000 *Britannia*, and this loco, together with preserved ex-LNER 'A3' No 4472 *Flying Scotsman* will haul two rail tours passing through Bolton en route for Morecambe from Stockport on Sunday 17 March.

During March 1968 my parents think I've adopted Bolton sheds as my second home, as I spend so much time there.

By 13 March the 'Belfast Boat Express' is drawing increasing numbers of enthusiasts travelling to see a steam-hauled passenger service still working – and how! 'Black Five' No 45017 keeps up the tradition of spirited departures from Trinity Street station on this cold, dark night, lit by dozens of flash guns from her appreciative audience. Why did I leave my camera at home?

Above: On Saturday 2 March 1968 Stanier 'Black Five' No 45104 has her smokebox cleared at Bolton sheds.

Below: 'Black Five' No 44947 simmers gently outside the sheds while awaiting her next duty, alongside BR 0-6-0 shunter No D3784.

Above: Representatives of the three principal classes of surviving locos wait outside the sheds. Left to right, they are 8F No 48111, BR Class 5 No 73069, and 'Black Five' No 45318.

Below: The controls of 'Black Five' No 45381 as she waits inside the sheds.

Above: One of the smartest-looking locos on shed on 2 March, BR Class 5 No 73069 reflects the early evening sunlight on Sunday 3 March.

Below: As the light fades, BR Class 5 No 73040 appears from the gloom of the sheds to take her next duty on 3 March.

'Last Days of Steam' rail tour

On Sunday 17 March 1968 the William Deacon's Bank 'Last Days of Steam' rail tour comes to Bolton.

The 20-yard-long queue for a souvenir platform ticket (priced, by the way, at 1 shilling, compared with the usual platform ticket rate of 1 penny) does nothing to deter the throng of eager 'nostalgics' forming the reception party that awaits the four locomotives on show

(22037)
SOUVENIR PLATFORM TICKET
"LAST DAYS OF STEAM"
Visit of
4472   70013
FLYING   OLIVER
SCOTSMAN   CROMWELL
Sunday, 17th March, 1968
STOCKPORT MANCHESTER (Victoria)
BOLTON
Charge 1s. 0d.
(M)   For conditions see over

today. Welcome visitors taking the two trains from Stockport to Carnforth and back are ex-LNER legend No 4472 *Flying Scotsman* and preserved 'Britannia' Class No 70013 *Oliver Cromwell*, each to be assisted by a 'Black Five' from Bolton sheds, Nos 45290 and 45110. Both main platforms are filling with excited children and their equally excited parents. First on the scene, and immaculately turned out, is No 45290, which has the honour of teaming up with *Flying Scotsman* for the outward journey and *Oliver Cromwell* for the return leg.

Not long after their departure, the second of Bolton's 'Black Fives', No 45110, rolls into the station to herald the arrival of the second 'star attraction'. Not to be outdone by her more famous forerunner, 'Britannia' Class No 70013 *Oliver Cromwell* storms to a halt. After uncoupling and moving forward, No 45110 takes her place at the head of the train, then *Oliver Cromwell* returns to take the leading role.

Above: Bolton's 'Black Five' No 45290 arrives at Trinity Street light engine to take the first of the 'Last Days of Steam' rail tours on 17 March.

Below: No 4472 *Flying Scotsman* arrives at the platform with her train.

Above: No 70013 *Oliver Cromwell* then brings her train into the station.

Below: The 'Britannia' uncouples to allow 'Black Five' No 45110 to reverse onto the train.

Both engines are now coupled at the head of the train, shortly to thunder out of the station.

Both locos securely 'double-headed', the second 'Last Days of Steam' special is ready to leave for Carnforth. Working as one, Nos 70013 and 45110 thunder out of the station amid clouds of smoke and with safety valves screaming. So ends the excitement for the morning, but tonight will hopefully bring a repeat performance on the return trips.

In the meantime, a visit to the sheds will occupy the afternoon nicely. There's plenty of interest on shed today, with 14 'Black Fives' present, Nos 44664, 44715, 44728, 44829, 44894, 44905, 44929, 44947, 45104, 45260, 45294, 45318, 45377 and 45381, of which sadly only Nos 45104 and 45318 are in steam. Thirteen 8Fs are present, Nos 48026, 48046, 48090, 48111, 48200, 48380, 48504, 48559, 48652, 48702, 48740, 48744 and 48764, of which only No 48026 is in steam. Also on shed and in steam are BR Class 5 Nos 73040 and 73069. Last, and by all means least, is one diesel shunter, No D2224.

BR Class 5 No 73040 waits peacefully in Bolton shed yard for her next duty.

Above: 8F No 48744 stands alongside the water crane.

Below: Alongside No 48744 are the back-ends of Nos 73069 and 45104.

8F No 48532 stands on the scrap line awaiting her final journey to the breaker's yard.

The scrap line is occupied by just three engines, all 8Fs, Nos 48465, 48469 and 48532.

Home to refuel myself, then tonight it's back to Trinity Street station in the hope of a repeat of the treats of this morning. The first steam on the scene in the evening is the Manchester-Heysham Harbour 'Belfast Boat Express', with 'Black Five' No 45025 enthusiastically driven as ever, but despite her powerful exit her glory is stolen by the double exhausts of Nos 70013 with 45290 in front of their returning train. The 'Black Five' is soon uncoupled and storms off towards the sheds, whistles blowing from both engines, soon after 9.20pm. No 70013 follows, wheels slipping, whistle blowing, steam bellowing and cameras flashing. Soon she is alongside the sheds and her whistle is echoed by every one of the locos who witness her passing.

A long wait follows, eventually rewarded with the arrival,

at 10.50pm, of the second 'special' with *Flying Scotsman* headed by her 'Black Five'. No 45110 is soon away to the sheds with the customary exchange of whistles, but No 4472 is having a problem. Maybe this accounts for her late running. Her vacuum brake refuses to release and it is not until 11.15pm that the problem is eventually solved and she thunders off belligerently into the night, whistling her way past the sheds towards Manchester.

What a day this has been – one that I am sure I and many more enthusiasts will never ever forget. Gradually the throng dissolves into the night, content with a glut of memories safely stored on film, but happier to have stood witness to the enduring power of these locomotives.

Thursday 21 March sees an unusual passing visitor to the sheds in the form of Carnforth 'Black Five' No 44874, looking in fine condition as might be expected from this depot. By 22 March two more locos have been added to the scrap line, both 8Fs, Nos 48090 and 48111. On the evening of 23 March a friend and I are given the opportunity to get close up and personal. With the aid of rags soaked in paraffin and lots of 'elbow grease', we had 'Black Five' No 45381 gleaming and looking fit for anything, satisfying hard work that was rewarded with a gift of a BR(M) oil-can as a memento of the occasion. It should clean up nicely and in years to come will be a reminder of all the happy hours I spent among these locomotives.

APRIL

The April 1968 edition of *The Railway Magazine* lists some interesting facts about the recent state of the steam scene, albeit dating from January. On 27 January 21 steam locomotives were listed as allocated to Stockport Edgeley depot (9B), 13 at Heaton Mersey (9F), 56 at Patricroft (26F, now re-coded as 9H) and 53 at Newton Heath (26A, now 9D). Stafford shed (5C) was home to 9F 2-10-0 No 92220 *Evening Star* and 'Black Five' No 45000, both scheduled for preservation. On the LMR, 30 steam locos are listed as withdrawn for the period to 27 January, of which 11 are 'Black Fives', 14 8Fs, three BR Class 5s and two 9Fs.

Bolton depot, now recoded as 9K, continues to receive a share of steam stock reallocated as a result of depot closures elsewhere. Recent additions are 'Black Five' Nos 44802, 44829 and 45294, together with 8F Nos 48046 and 48200. All welcome!

Carlisle Kingmore (12A), Workington (12F) and Tebay (12H) depots are listed as closed completely from 1 January, while Carlisle now boasts a new diesel depot known simply as Carlisle and coded 12A, opened for business on the same date. It is also interesting to note that BR is reported as having withdrawn its original five 'Warship' class diesel-hydraulics, Nos D600-D604, which were introduced in 1958. BR considers these locomotives to be life-expired at ten years old!

April 1968 brings more cold weather, but visiting Bolton sheds is still a regular source of steam-inspiration. One such visit, on 2 April, reveals 8F No 48469, long since retired to the scrap line (see page 104), is actually being cut up here on site, presumably as she is now considered unsafe to move.

Above: On 2 April 1968 No 48469's boiler casing has been removed and she is disembowelled, her pipework lying in a heap nearby.

Below: By 5 April the locomotive has been cut into pieces and her central portion, including the remains of her boiler, have been removed.

Above: On 8 April only the tender remains, a lonely sight.

Below: Not all is gloom and doom, though. Elsewhere in the sheds it's business as usual. Stanier 8F Nos 48702 and, beyond, 48465 poke their noses out from the sheds on 8 April 1968.

Above: Stanier 'Black Fives' in steam are Nos 44829 and, beyond, 44947, the former being one of our new allocation.

'Black Five' No 45095, Standard Class 5 No 73069 and, in the background, No 45290 simmer gently outside the sheds as the recent light snowfall melts around them.

Still quite clean after our efforts of a couple of weeks ago, 'Black Five' No 45381 leaves the coaling tower ready for work.

Before taking an Easter break in the Lake District, I've time to squeeze in one more visit to Bolton sheds via Trinity Street station. Here 8F No 48033 enters Bolton Trinity Street station with a mixed goods train.

The pair of 'Black Fives' that so ably assisted *Flying Scotsman* and *Oliver Cromwell* recently, Nos 45290 and 45110, pose outside the sheds while waiting their next turns.

Further across the entrance to the sheds, 8F No 48504 stands alongside another of Bolton's 'Black Fives', No 45260.

MAY

End of the line for the 'Belfast Boat Express'

The Manchester-Heysham Harbour daily connecting service for the ferry to Belfast is probably the last regular steam-hauled passenger express running on British Rail. However, nothing is safe from the march of 'progress', and on Sunday 5 May 1968 this train will make its last run with steam in charge.

The day before we cannot let the occasion pass without paying our final farewells to a piece of railway history. We

No 45342 at the head of the penultimate steam-hauled 'Belfast Boat Express'. [*M. Smith*

join a throng on Bolton's Trinity Street station platform. A couple of friends and myself will ride this penultimate train as far as Preston, as we have done on so many superb evenings in the past. As the time approaches, a hundred ears strain for the sound of exhaust beats thundering past the sheds towards the station. We are not disappointed. Carnforth 'Black Five' No 45342 storms into view, boasting a fine headboard and looking a picture.

Many enthusiasts have turned out at Bolton to watch and photograph the spectacle and many more are waiting at Preston as we arrive after an exhilarating race through the darkness, steam, smoke, sparks flying, whistle screaming along the main line for almost the final time. All agreed, a great run.

The last 'Belfast Boat Express' behind steam. [*M. Smith*

Next day, Sunday 5 May – the last one. Fittingly, another Carnforth 'Black Five' has the honour, though speculation was that *Oliver Cromwell* or *Ayrshire Yeomanry* would be given the run. Tonight, countless enthusiasts line Trinity Street's platforms and the darkness is broken by innumerable flashes from scores of cameras. Stanier's workhorses have done this express proud, and for the last time No 45025 fills the station with the familiar smells of smoke and burning coal. Then she's off into the night, and we faithful are left, bereft, as the gasps and sighs of the last steam-hauled 'Belfast Boat Express' fade away.

Since that day, the train has been unceremoniously hauled by 'Brush 4' diesels, provoking no interest on its nightly passage through Bolton. Meanwhile we do have the sheds operating normally, and are still receiving allocations of locomotives from elsewhere, as other depots are closed to steam, but realistically even they cannot last for long, as the announcement of the date I have been dreading hearing is finally made public. Bolton engine sheds will officially close on 1 July 1968.

JULY

For the first time in my memory, the gates to Bolton sheds are closed, but oddly, I find, not locked. The locos are still here, silent as the grave. One railwayman still has a job here for the time being. His role is to watch over the shed and its contents until breaking-up time comes. He has no problem with us few enthusiasts who come to pay our respects, though he too appears almost overcome with the poignancy of the scene.

'They're all dead,' are his only words.

1 July 1968. Gates closed…

Locos in the sheds at the time of closure are Stanier 'Black Five' Nos 44664, 44802, 44829, 44888, 44929, 44947, 45046, 45104, 45260, 45290, 45312 and, not so clean now, 45381. These are joined by No 45110 some days later, though she mysteriously disappears again soon after and is rumoured to be scheduled to take part in the 'Final Steam Train' special excursion in August, perhaps along with *Oliver Cromwell*, and then both may be preserved. 8Fs on shed are Nos 48026, 48168, 48319, 48380, 48392, 48504, 48652, 48692, 48702 and 48720. A total of 22 steam locomotives, and four worn-out Drewry 0-6-0 diesel shunters, introduced in 1955, Nos D2224, D2226, D2227 and D2234, await the cutter's torch.

The local press takes up the story. The *Bolton Evening News*, 10 July 1968 has the headline 'Farewell to age of steam'. A day later, 'Last respects at the silent sheds'.

AUGUST

The End of Steam

Well, it's finally arrived. The day I dreaded. The day I would see steam working on a BR passenger service for the last time. It's 11 August 1968, the day BR has decreed will be the end of steam on the network. A couple of enthusiast friends and myself arrive at Manchester Victoria station at 10.10am, expecting to be able to see the first stage of the special train from Liverpool Lime Street, due to be hauled by a Stanier 'Black Five', possibly Bolton's own No 45110, then watch the scheduled change of engines to allow 'Britannia' No 70013 *Oliver Cromwell* to take charge for the trip up to Carlisle.

Getting a sight of the locos turns out to be more problematic than it sounds. Virtually no attempt has been made to cater in any way for the massive gathering that has converged on Victoria station. The result is mass confusion, frustration and not a little anger.

What to do?

We decide that our best course of action is to make a dash back to Bolton in the hope of getting a view from some less-populated vantage point at Trinity Street station. Many people have turned out here too, but at 11.28am, just 1 minute late, No 70013 makes her appearance. There is much clapping and clicking of camera shutters as the train, hampered by the 20mph speed restriction through the station, trundles past and out towards Castle Hill and the Blackburn line. I am overcome with disappointment at this lacklustre performance. I remember this same loco bringing the crowd to life earlier in the year. No whistles, no safety valves screaming, no slipping wheels, not even a photo-stop.

139

Above: Manchester Victoria, 11 August 1968. The frontage of the ex-L&YR station.

Left: Inside the station is a plaque in remembrance of employees who gave their lives in the First World War.

Everyone files out of the station with barely a word being exchanged, no doubt hoping, as I am, that the return leg this evening will bring a better show. And what a spectacle it brings.

I take up a position opposite Bolton East signal box, near the Orlando Street footbridge. Here the train should be picking up speed after negotiating the speed restriction

'Britannia' Class No 70013 *Oliver Cromwell* passes through Bolton Trinity Street station on her last trip from Liverpool to Carlisle, 11 August 1968.

through Trinity Street station. It's 6.45pm and she is due in Manchester Victoria at 6.48pm! There's no sign of her. Suddenly the signals are pulled off and all senses are strained in anticipation. The train is scheduled to be hauled by 'double-headed' 'Black Fives' for the return trip and we all wait expectantly at the prospect of a spirited race to make up time. 6.50pm. The unmistakeable sound of distant steam engines causes a buzz of excitement as the locos can be heard rounding the curves through Trinity Street station. Then, as they enter the straight, both drivers open up their locomotives as one when they see they have a clear road. Whistles and steam mingle with cheers from the crowd as they thunder past, accelerating quickly towards the sheds and Manchester, leaving us bathed in familiar clouds of smoke and sulphurous exhaust. What a fitting finale –

Below and opposite: 'Black Fives' in tandem: Nos 44871 and 44781 accelerate away from Trinity Street station and under Orlando Bridge with the penultimate leg of BR's last-ever steam-hauled train.

Stanier 'Black Fives', often hailed as the best all-purpose locomotives ever built, stating the case so powerfully that the end is horribly premature.

Sister loco No 45305 will take the last leg from Manchester to Liverpool, a fitting end to the era of steam.

Once again the local press was there to record the scenes for posterity. The *Bolton Evening News* of 12 August reported: 'Cameras click farewell to steam age as the last train pants by'. The 'nationals' also recorded the historic event; on Saturday 10 August the *Daily Express* had 'Steaming beauty gets spick and span funeral' and the Daily Telegraph, 'Steam lovers' "sentimental journey".'

• • •

On Monday 12 August I have to do this – pay one last visit to Bolton sheds. Some of the locos have already gone, including cherished 'Black Five' Nos 44888 and 45260, but a total of 19 steam locomotives remain, plus yet another doomed 0-6-0 diesel shunter, No D2373.

After 34 years of service, Stanier 'Black Five' No 45104 stands silently outside Bolton sheds awaiting her final journey.

Above: Sister loco No 44947 stands by a water tower. Both are redundant.

Below: Two Stanier 8Fs stand coupled together in deathly silence. Nos 48652 and 48319 wait to be towed away.

Looking past 'dead' No 44947 towards the coaling stage, which dispensed life-giving fuel to the ever-hungry locos. Now all is still. No coal, no steam, no life.

Beyond 'dead' 8F No 48319 can be seen an example of the motive power that is the replacement for so much of the passenger steam stock, the diesel multiple unit.

Epilogue to steam

August 1968. I can hardly believe that in the space of one short year we have seen the demise of the last of the nation's steam locomotives. One year ago, my friend and I felt the joy of an epic run up to Lancaster behind 'Britannia' *Owen Glendower*, photographed nine 'Britannia' Class locos in one day and used up countless frames of film shooting 'Black Fives', 8Fs and 9Fs between Wigan North Western and Lancaster stations. One year ago I was mourning the loss to the Southern of their last 'Pacifics' – 'Merchant Navy', 'Battle of Britain' and 'West Country' classes – to the 'Eastern', their Gresley 'A4s' and 'B1s', little comprehending that just 12 months later I would have said goodbye not only to steam traction on the West Coast route, but also to the total steam fleet on British Railways.

But technology progresses and no amount of sentimental writing will prevent the rise of the diesel era. We must salute the end of the steam age and accept that the kings have finally been deposed. Mercifully the campaign to preserve some locos is gaining pace, but for the vast majority it's a case of 'farewell old friends', and bring on the next generation...

Above right: The next generation: E-E Type 4 No D340 passes Bolton East Junction signal box with a parcels train.

Right: With steam now gone, it remains only to record some of the railway features in and around Bolton, which in time will surely also become surplus to requirements. This L&YR notice near Bolton warns that 'persons in charge of locomotive traction engines and other ponderous carriages' should not pass over the bridge.

Lostock Junction signal box, on the route of the 'Belfast Boat Express'.

Part of Bolton Trinity Street station, including the Station signal box.

Bolton's Trinity Street station approaches are protected by two fine signal boxes. This view of the approach to the station shows the footbridge and Bolton West signal box.

Above: This is Bolton East signal box and Orlando Bridge.

Below: Next to the station stands the impressive building of the 'London Midland and Scottish Railway Goods Warehouse'.

The impressive signals of Burnden Junction.

Above: Burnden Junction signal box.

Below: Signal wire pulleys and lineside debris alongside Burnden Junction signal box.

Diesels triumph at Bolton East: a DMU approaches Bolton East signal box after leaving Trinity Street station.

A DMU passes Bolton East signal box, with the floodlights of Burnden Park football ground, home of Bolton Wanderers, in the background.

An English Electric Type 4 takes a parcels train towards Manchester.

EPILOGUE: 40 YEARS ON

It is now 2008. Forty years have elapsed since the end of steam on British Rail. At that time, it seemed the final curtain had fallen and the widely held view was that steam locomotives would never again haul their trains over the nation's railways. But the preservation movement grew ever more powerful and eventually the anti-steam lobby relented, or saw commercial opportunities in the steam nostalgia business.

Today, the UK and Ireland boast more than 170 'Heritage Railway' sites, with almost 100 railways offering regular passenger trains, over 80 of which are standard gauge lines. Happily, many cherished locos have survived, lovingly preserved and restored to grace the tracks again, bringing

Stanier 'Black Five' No 5407 hurries towards Long Preston with the 'Cumbrian Mountain Express' in October 1983.

Stanier 'Coronation' Class No 45229 *Duchess of Hamilton* leaves Garsdale in October 1985.

back memories of steam's former glory. Even more significantly, steam-hauled specials now regularly operate on the main lines, including over the once threatened masterpiece of railway engineering, the awesome Settle and Carlisle route, as can be seen in the accompanying photographs.